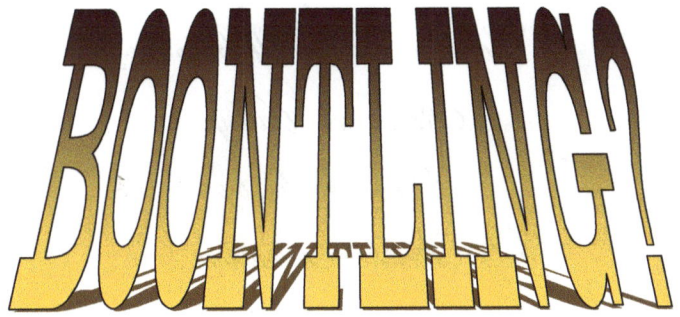

Cover photos are all from the
Anderson Valley.
Photography by
Judy Belshe-Toernblom © 2007

3nd Edition

Copyright 2007 by Judy Belshe-Toernblom. All rights reserved.

The entire contents of this edition of "English to Boontling" is copyrighted. No part of the publication may be reproduced in any form, or stored in a database or retrieval system, or transmitted or distributed in any form by any means, electronic, mechanical photocopying, recording, or otherwise in English or any other language without the prior written permission of the author.
DISCLAIMER:
The author has taken all reasonable measures to insure the accuracy of the information in this edition of "English to Boontling." However, the information contained in this publication is provided AS IS, without warranty of any kind, expressed or implied, and neither publisher nor the author can accept responsibility for any errors or omissions, or assume any liability resulting from the use, or inability to use, or misuse of any of the information or materials contained herein. In no event shall the publisher or the author be liable for direct, indirect, special, incidental, or consequential damages arising out of the use of or inability to use this publication.

I would like to extend my gratitude to the following people who helped in my research for this book and the coming novel:

Sheri Hansen
Jeff "Spiffy" Burroughs
Donald Wes "Deekin" Smoot
Don "Ite" Pardini
Walter "Shine" Tuttle
Edna Beth Tuttle
James "Bo" Hiatt
Bobbie "Wee Bo" Hiatt
Catherine Nobles Sinnott
Tim Mathias
J. Robert Mathias
Clyde Price
And most of all my wonderful husband Birger.
He is my awesome partner who goes with me on every adventure at a moments notice!
Tries to corrects all my typing and spelling errors.
And loves me and all my crazy ideas.

"English to Boontling"

By Judy Belshe-Toernblom © 2007

The catchy language of Boontling was born as a spoken language in Northern California in the area of Bell Valley and Boonville.

If you happened on to this town on your own back in 1960s this local who had a few questions, statements and directions might have greeted you. In an article in the magazine called, The Nation, in 1969, there was just such a happening.

A car had broken down and its occupants needed a place to stay and the car needed some repair. They met a man named Phocian McGimsey, but everybody called him "Levi". He was 73 at the time. This is what he had to say:

"You piked to boont in your moshe geekin' on a moshe?" he said. "Moshe's strung, kimmie, but pike in the nook an' whittle a slib by the jeffer. Got enough zeese for a gormin' tidric. You from Belk? There's a nonch sluggin' nook ye can pike to," he said and gestured up the road.

At the end of the book come back and I just bet you'll know what he said. This is just one of the many stories about this language and the fun-loving hearts and minds of people in this area.

I do wish I'd been around with Chipmunk and Deekin' when they were sitting around talking in Boont.

In an article by Russell Johnson called "Befuddled in Boonville" he captured one of those very conversations.

Chipmunk went to the hob. "I shied the hob," harped Deekin', "too codgy." "There was a huge fister," harped Chipmunk, "and the highman of the higheelers brought in thribs deputies and shut 'er down." "Not bahl," harped Deekin. Chipmunk said, "Gotta have a fister once in awhile to get it out of yer system."

Translation:

Chipmunk went to the dance. Deekin' didn't, "getting too old for that," he said. Chipmunk said " there was a big fight and the sheriff brought in three deputies to shut it down." "Not good," said Deekin'. Chipmunk said, "you got to have a fight once in a while to get it out of your system."

My fascination with this language continued to grow and I began exploring it more. After our visit to Boonville, California I returned to our home in Southern California and wrote the screenplay, "Boonville Redemption."

In the script Boontling is used to open communication between a young girl and her grandmother and it also helps to solve a mystery.

But I wanted more; I had to return to Boonville. This time I wanted to do more research in order to write a novel based on the screenplay. In order to do just that I had to create for myself a larger and more complete English to Boontling dictionary.

When we returned to Boonville, much to my delight there were people who still loved to talk about the stories and speak Boontling.

From this research has emerged this "English to Boontling" book. I truly believe if an active attempt is not made to write this language down the joy of this lingo will die on the lips of the last Boonter.

I found it so helpful to hear the stories of how some words were developed. Most words are an amalgamation of two or more words. Once you know the words, the Boontling word will make sense. Once you've learned a word and the reason behind it, you'll own it.

Most all of the words have a story about their development. That is what is so unique about this regional language. It's attached to the people of this area and their lives at that time. I will endeavor wherever possible to repeat these stories and meaning to you.

A common mistake is to think you must say the entire sentence in Boontling. Boontling is like a delicious verbal spice that tickles your ear as it is sprinkled throughout a sentence. You know you are hearing English, you don't know what is being said, but you like it!

This book endeavors to spell the words closest to familiar pronunciation. In some cases there are various spellings to get to the pronunciation accurate.

I also discovered in my research that some of the words have more than one spelling and or meaning, just like several words of your everyday English.

I've tried to choose words that you would use in your everyday life. It's my goal to make learning Boontling easier for you so you'll use it and share it. I hope this book accomplishes this purpose. I want to do my part to keep this language alive for the beloved people of Boonville, those who created it and those yet to discover it.

Don "Ite" Pardini once said in an article in the San Francisco Chronicle:

> **We've all piked for dusties now,**
>
> **our harpin' days are gone.**
>
> **But we'll never be teebow,**
>
> **if Boont is pikin'on.**

Which translates:

> **We've all gone to the cemetery now,**
> **our speaking days are gone.**
> **But we'll never be deaf,**
> **if Boontling is carried on.**

*I would like to add to this book with each printing. So if you have a Boontling word that you think needs to be included in this book please feel free to contact me at: **JudyBelshe@aol.com**.*

My wish for Boonville, you the reader and the generations that are to come is that you will keep on HARPIN' BOONTLING!

Abalone chaser: **AB CHASER**
This name was given for people that lived on the coast.

Accident: **BLOOD 'N HAIR**
*The expression was derived from what it looked like at a scene of a bad accident. "It was a **NONCH BLOOD'N HAIR**."*

Adultery: **BRANCHIN' or FENCE JUMPIN'**
It means that you've branched out, jumped over your wedded fence, gone outside the marital commitment. Use it in a sentence. ***Thou shalt not commit BRANCHIN'.***

Aggressive person: **BEARK**
*Skillful shaping of the word 'bear cat.' "We saw an 'ol **BEARK** stalking a **CROPPY**."*

Albion: **ABALONE**
A beautiful coastal community that was once a mill town and rival of Boonville.

Alcoholic: **HIGH GITTER or SILENT HORNER or TINKLER**

***HIGH GITTER** is someone who gets drunk on a regular basis. A **SILENT HORNER** is someone who drinks alone or in secret. The following story was told to me by Wes "Deekin" Smoot about the word **TINKLER**. A woman was talking on the phone. The entire time she could hear the person rattle the ice cubes in their drink. So when she got off the phone she told her husband that the person that she was talking to was a **TINKLER** and that is how this particular Boontling word was coined.*

Alcohol
(going to get some secretly)   **PIKE TO THE TURKEY SHACK**

During prohibition the Doctor in the town could get medicines that were laced with alcohol and all kinds of stuff. When he'd get in the shipment he would go out to his turkey shack and hang a lantern out and everyone would know he had the alcohol. So there'd be a line out there at the turkey shack in the middle of the night to get alcohol, "for medicinal purposes" of course. (As told by Jeff "Spiffy" Burroughs)

Alcohol-free: **ITCH NEEMER**
When a person no longer craves alcohol. They no longer have the "Itch" to drink.

All or everything: **HEELCH**
A large quantity, or the whole amount of something. Think of the saying, "The whole cheese."

Angry: **BOW ON**
To become angry with, challenge to fight. Also used for when a guy was sweet on a girl.

Angry #2:   **COCK / COCKED**
A hairpin anger that goes off quick like a cocked gun.

Angry #3:   **CAN KICKER**
Ever get angry and just start kicking a can down the street? This expression came from that action.

Angry #2:   **TEET-LIPPED**
Pouting or the pressing of your lips tight like when you are mad.

Anytime(The), or Anyhow(The):
(anehou) (aniyhaw)
*This was a well-known saloon built between
Boonville and Yorkville. It was just outside the
Boonville School District. The 'dry' laws were
passed in 1906 and the saloon was closed. But the
local drinkers were determined to have it "Anyhow,"
so they moved the building outside the boundary
and named it the "Anyhow." Making a bold
statement that they were going to drink ANYHOW!
The building now resides in Philo, California as
Libby's Restaurant.*

Apple: **GANNO or
GANNOW or
GANO**

This was a Spanish apple.

Apple dryer: **APPELDER or
APELDER**

*Some of the apples raised in Anderson Valley were
dried in large barns designed for drying apples.
The Boonville museum has a replica of an
apple dryer barn on display.*

Apple exhibit
aka Apple Show: **APPEELSH or APELSH**

An apple exhibit named after the Mendocino County Fair held in Boonville each fall.

Apron: **MOSSY**

This can also can mean to 'change subjects.' Mossy (the woman this was named after) was known to change the subject in the middle of a conversation.

Area, geographical place: **REGION**

Arkansas immigrant: **ARKER**
They could be from the upper South or the Midwest.

Arrest: **HIGH HEEL**

Arrested (to be):   **HIGH HEELED**

Arresting police officer: **HIGH HEELER**
Origin of this word is, the constable of that time had one leg shorter than the other so he wore a boot that was high-heeled.

Ass or Buttocks: **OSE**
*"I've fallen on my **OSE** and can't get up!"*

Ate: **GORMED**
*"I **GORMED** the whole bag of **BOO** chips."*

Attractive woman: **BAHLNESS**
A very extraordinarily beautiful woman. This is a very high compliment.

Bachelor: **BATTER**
*Could mean that he's a single guy still up to bat **DEEKIN'** for a **DAME**. That's how I choose to memorize it.*

Bachelor's Cabin: **BATTER SHACK**

Backwards or Backwoodsy: **RIDGY**
*Can also mean old or decrepit. "That bridge looks too **RIDGY** to cross."*

Backwards person: **BACKDATED CHUCK**
It can also mean ill-informed, naïve or stupid.

Bacon: **BOWRP**

Here is sleeping place, fire, bacon and eggs used in a sentence.

"If I don't shy to the sluggin' region soon, I may as well set me a jeffer and gorm bowrp and Easters."

Bad Deal: **ROOJIN'**

It's like the expression, "I was rooked!"

Bad, not good: **NEEBLE or NONCH**

It can also mean inferior or defective.

Bad Language: **NONCH HARPIN'**

*Meaning bad talking or talking bad. "Billy was put in the corner for **NONCH HARPIN'**."*

Bald Hills: **THE BALDIES**

The high hills northeast of Boonville.

Bank: **HIGGERY or ITE VAULT**

This is referring to the Italian families that were involved with the Bank of America.

Bar: **HORNIN' REGION**

Any place where a person could get an alcoholic drink.

Barber: **HEDGER**
Makes your hair sound rather organic doesn't it?

Baseball: **BUZZ CHICK**
This is a word that is based on the sound the ball made when it was pitched and then caught in the catcher's mitt.

Bear: **LEEBER**

Bear dung or
Berry cobbler (pie): **BEARTRACK**
This word mean BOTH so be careful what you ask for in a restaurant!

Bear location
and Berry location: **LEEBER REGION**

Beat or Whip: **JOE MACK, also LARRUP, DREEK**
Named after a local scrapper named Joe McGimsey.

Beaten: **DREEKED**
*"He was **DREEKED** nearly to death."*

Beating or Whipping: **DREEKIN'**
*"He took a **NONCH DREEKIN'**."*

Bedroom: **SLUGGIN' NOOK**
*A beautiful Boontling toast using the words **SLUGGIN' NOOK**, goes like this:*
    Wee turteel, bahl neemershay
    Til your wee hobs and my weehobs
    In the sluggin' nook are kip.

Beer: **STEINBER**
Stein like in a German beer stein and the shortening of the word beer to ber.

Bell Valley: **BELK REGION**
This is a quiet scenic valley located just beyond the Baldies, northeast of Boonville.

It was here in the hop fields, during the turn of the century, that the language of Boontling originated. My husband and I visited the beautiful Toll House on our last visit. Across from the Toll House the weary travelers used to be able to refresh themselves a their horses at the soda creek.
Bell Valley got its name because the wagons that traveled down the hills had bells on them and the drivers would ring the bells as a notice to the other travelers as they hauled the hops to market. This let the people coming in the opposite direction know they were on the same road.

Bell Valley

Belk Region

This is the area where they grew the hops and the birthplace of "Boontling."

Belligerent or Cocky: **FEATHERLEG**
Like the banty rooster that likes to fight.

Better or Best: **BAHLER**
*There was a brand of shoe that had a RED BALL on the sole. If you owned of pair of these shoes you had the best there was. So the expression of BALL began to mean all things good or best. It is often spelled **BAHL** in Boont.*

Bible: **BIG BOOK**

Big: **HUGER**

Big (extremely):   **SOCKER**
*"That **SEERTLE** was **SOCKER**!"*

Biscuit (light-bread):   **FLORIES**
*This word was coined after a woman named FLORA, who was said to have the best biscuits in the valley. So if you were eating one of her biscuits you would be **"GORMING a BAHL FLORIE."***

Biscuit /Soda: **LOWEEZIES**
Loweezie or Wiese's Valley Inn was a very popular Restaurant in Boonville. The biscuit was rumored to be named after the woman Louisa who made them. I'm not sure if she owned the restaurant of the same name or if they both just made great biscuits!

Black Sheep: **JEANSHEEP**
There was a local black man who lived in Boonville whose last name was Jeans. The origin of this word could have come from that.

Book: **BOK**

Bookkeeper: **BOOKEY**
Bookkeeper by occupation.

Boonville Cemetery: **BOONT DUSTY**
*"Many of the **BOONTLINGERS** have **PIKED** to the **BOONT DUSTY**." The tenants would be the **BOONT DUSTIES**.*

Boonville Cemetary

Boont Dusty

Brain or to think: **GREYMATTER**

There is some good advice that was given by Bob "Chipmunk" Glover on using your brain. He is quoted in the Mendocino Mushroom Forager issue for 1980 (the "Boont Ite-Steak Greeley Sheet") in Boont. He is warning about mushrooms and knowing the difference between the good ones and the bad ones. He was an expert in this area. Here is the quote Bob "Chipmunk" Glover said. Now it's up to you to figure out the meaning:

"You must do much graymatterin' fore pikin' for seekin' Ite steaks to gorm, cause the sockers might not be bahlers, but nonchers with dusties dust, so deek your bok well."

Broke: **DEHIGGED**

*Means you are without money/poor ."I went to Vegas **HIGHPOCKETY** but came back **DEHIGGED**."*

Bucked: **BLUE-BIRDED**

"Bucked off a horse." The name came from a story of a young man who was bucked off a horse. He said, "I got thrown so high that a blue bird could have built a nest on my butt."

Burp: **ALMITTEY or ALMIE**

To burp. A burp, especially a loud one. This was the name for a local woman who made consistent jarring burps.

Business: **LOW DESK or LOW DESKIN'**

Or simply put, just doing business.

Butt in or crowd: **ABE**

Buttocks: **BEE'N or BEEUN**

Smushing of the word "behind."

Candy: **DOOLSEY or DULCEY**

Can also be used to say sweet or sugar.

Candy making session: **DOOLSEY TIDRIC**

Camp revival: **SKYPIN' or SKIPIN'**

Also means a meeting or a sermon.

Cap or Hat: **KAYDEE**

Car: **MOSHE**
See machine.

Card game: **BUCKEY DUSTER**

This is a card game where nickels are used for betting.

Cap or Hat

Kaydee

**This hat was owned by Nancy Elizabeth Wallach McGimsey
Now displayed at the Anderson Valley Historical Museum.**

Cards/to play: **NICKELONK**
*Expression: I'm **NICKELONKED**. Out of nickels to play with.*

Carnival: **HURDY-GURDY**

Cat: **PUSSEEK**
This would be for a female domesticated cat.

Cemetery: **DUSTIES**

Chain saw: **SCRATCHER**
I know scratch sounds harmless but leave the guard on!

Change the subject: **MOSSY**
This can also can mean 'apron.' Mossy (the woman this was named after) was known to change the subject in the middle of a conversation.

Charge: **RAMPS**
It can also be used to say lunge or take a run at something.

Chatter aimlessly: **BLOOCH or BLOOCHER**
Anyone who chatters or goes on and on talking nonsense. Also a drunk talking nonsense.

Cheat: **ROOJE**
The expression "I was rooked" helps with this word.

Cheat or crowd out: **DISH**

Chicken or any fowl: **DOM or DOMINECKER**

*"The eternal question is, which came first, the **DOMINECKER** or the **EASTER**?"*

Child: **CHUCK**
An unruly child.

Child (small):   **TWEED or WEECH**

Taken from the expression wee suck. Also a sweet thing to call a child.

Child   **BULRUSHER**
This means a foundling or illegitimate child. Moses was found in the bulrushes and look, he turned out okay!

Childish: **TWEEDISH**
*"Rosie, Donald, don't be so **TWEEDISH!**"*

Chinese (Male):   **BOARCH**
A version of the word boar.

Church (large): **KINGSTER or SKYPE REGION, SKIPE REGION**

*See **SKIPE** or **SKYPE** for full explanation.*

United Methodist Church in Anderson Valley

Cider, hard: **PRICE BABCOCK**
This cider is aptly named after the local man and creator of the cider.

Cigarette: **CIG or SIG**
Shortening of the word cigarette. Ironic that they'd shorten the word to something that shortens your life!

City resident: **BRIGHT-LIGHTER**
Ah...that would be me the city girl!

Clothes: **SHODS**
This would be clothing of poor quality.

Clothing store: **CLOUT SALE**

Clouds   **FLEECIES**
It means large white puffy clouds which appear shortly after a rain storm. The reason for this is because they resemble large bundles of freshly sheared sheep wool, bundled up ready for sacking.

Coast dweller: **ABALONEYITE or FOG EATER**

Cocky or Belligerent: **FEATHERLEG**
This is in reference to the Banty Rooster.

Coffee: **ZEESE**

Not just coffee, coffee you could float an egg on. Z.C. "Zeese" Blivans was the maker of that strong coffee.

Coins or small change: **SMEELCH or SMALCH**

Game: Try saying small change really fast and smush the words!

Cold: **FRIGID**

Collect or collector: **CHIPMUNK**

Bob "Chipmunk" Glover comes to mind. He collected many things. He was also famous for his bottle collection and his knowledge of mushrooms. The meaning of the word is to collect or hoard. "He takes the shavings of his pencil and saves 'em," Wes "Deekin'" Smoot once said jokingly in an article by Vicki Haddock.

Come one, come all: **KEEMWUN KEEMLE**

Comprehend, Understand: **UNDERST**

Confused: **JIMHEADY**

*"When I first heard Boontling I was so **JIMHEADY!**"*

Contest: **MATCH**

It's funny that match would mean a contest when what you really want to do is win, not match. A match would be the beginning to see who comes out of the match the winner.

Cooked: **JEFFERED**

*Pioneer Jeff Vestal kept a roaring fire in his Missouri Hotel in Boonville at all times. So fire became known as a "**JEFFER.**"*

Courting: **PUT 'N ON**

Cow: **BROADIE or BROADEY**

Given this name because of their broad horns.

Cow bell: **DINKLEHONK**

Coined after the sound the bell makes.

Cowboy or Cowboy boots: **BARNEY MAN or ROOPEY BARNEYS**

There was a local named Barney. He only wore cowboy boots no matter what the season was!

Coyote: **BOOTJACK also KAI**

The coyote ears resembled the common tool for removing boots.

Crazy or wild: **CRAYZEEK or TUDDISH**

Going Crazy: **SHY TIGINESS**

Criticize: **NON ON**

Crowd in or push: **AB**

Cupboard is bare: **CHIGGRUL NOOK IS STRUNG**

One of my favorite poem using these Boontling words is the "Old Mother Hubbard" poem.
***The old dame piked for the chigrel nook
For gorms for her belljeemer.
The gorms had shied, the nook was strung,
And the bahl belljeemer had neemer.***

Dance or Shoe: HOB

*This is for a normal everyday shoe. There is another term for a heavier shoe called a **CLOUDY**.*

Dancer: HOBBER

Dance, to: HOBNEELCH

Dance Hall: HOBNEELCH REGION or HOB REGION

There is a town called Hopland if you liked dancing that was the town to go to.

Dancing: HOBBIN'

Die / Day: DEE

Dead/Died: DEED

Dating: DAMIN'

Dating and or going with different girl

Deer: BOSHE
This is taken from the Pomo Indian word bishe. Bishe or Belshe? I wonder if I'm related, I've been called a dear.

Deer Dog or hound: BOSHE HAREEM

Deer or deer hunting: BOSHIN' TIDRICS
Can also be used to say a deer hunting trip. Combination of the words, deer hunting, meeting, affair or get together. It's okay for your man to go on them as long as he comes back with a four legged deer and not a two legged kind.

Deer hunter: BOSHER

Degenerate: DEEGER or DEEJY DEEGY

Deserted or Lonely: DOVY-COOEY
*"It gets mighty **DOVY-COOEY** in the **COW SKULLY REGION.**"*

Desolate area: COW SKULLY
If you've ever traveled the old west you've seen your share of cow skulls in the desolate areas.

Die / Day: **DEE**

Different or odd: **HOOD**
*There was a family that moved to the region and the children wore hoods all day. The locals thought that was odd. So they coined the term for odd as **HOOD** or **HOODY**.*

Dime: **DEEM or MOLLY**
*Molly is a mixed meaning word. It can be a dime, doe deer or woman's breast. As in nice **MOLLIES**!*

Doctor: **SHOVELTOOTH**
This is a name for any Doctor. The first doctor of region had prominent, projecting teeth.

Dog: **HAIREEM**
This word is formed from two words, "Hairy and Mouth."

Doing the right thing: **FAIR 'N RIGHT**

Dollar: **BELHOON or HIG**
*A **BELHOON** is a paper dollar. **HIG** is mostly used when talking about the silver dollar.*

Donkey or Mule: JEEKUS
Also the word for Brandy because a local brandy was called Jackass Brandy. This can also refer to anyone that acts like a jackass.

Dog

Haireem

Double / Two of anything: **DUBS**

Doubtful / worrisome: **SKIDDLEY**

Drink: **HORN**
*In the early days animal horns were used to hold drinks. This word refers to any drinking item, cup etc. Remember, "If you **HORN** don't **JAPE**."*

Drinker: **HORNER**
This would be a hard liquor drinker.

Drinker: **SILENT HORNER**
This would be a secret drinker.

Drive: **JAPE**
*Here's drive and egg in a sentence together. It's also good advice. "Put an **EASTER** under your foot and **JAPE** safely."*

Driver of the car: **JAPER**
*" I'm a very **BAHL JAPER**." Dustin Hoffman/Rainman. If he were a Boonter.*

Drunk: **HIGH**

Drunk (Very):   **HIGHER 'N BILLY**
*Other expressions are: **HIGHER 'N BOLLEY'S FIDDLE** and **HIGHER 'N DWIGHT'S FLAGPOLE.***

There was a gent that when he got drunk always ended up sleeping it off at the Boonville flagpole. You guessed it, his name was Dwight!
Wes "Deekin" Smoot and Don "Ite" Pardini told me the story of Bolley's Fiddle. A classical music company came to town one day and Bolley heard them play. Well, they were so good that he vowed to never play his fiddle again. So he hung it high and there is where it stayed.

Drunkenness: **HIGH GITTIN'**

Dull-witted: **CHUCKISH**
                                         also CHUCKEY
This can also mean mentally slow. There was a local that was mentally slow and they coined the word after his name.

Dynamite: **TROJAN**
There was a brand named dynamite in those days called, "Trojan Dynamite."

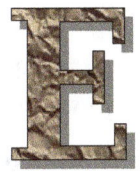

Eavesdrop: **RUBBERNECK**
This also meant to listen in on a party line. I'm old enough to remember the party line! Rubbernecking has stretched its definition to qualify for the freeways now.

Earth: **TRUTH**
*"It's not nice to fool Mother **TRUTH**."*

Eat too much: **GORM, CHIGGLE, CHIGGRUL, and CHIGGREL**
A Combination of the words, chew gruel.
*"I can't believe I **GORMED** the **HEELCH!**"*

Edge someone out: **MONK**
This also means to take the deal away from someone. This word is coined after a local Boonter named Monk. He was reportedly a very assertive businessman.

Egg or Eggs: **EASTER or EASTERS**

This is such a cute way to say eggs.

Elementary School: **WEE HEESE**

Embarrass or to embarrass: **CHARLIE BALL or CHARLIE BALLED Or CHARLIE**

This word was coined after a local Indian named Charlie Ball. He was bashful and easy to embarrass.

Enjoy repeatedly: **BOARCH**

To enjoy anything repeatedly. It was noticed that the early Chinese road-workers loved to see entertaining things over and over. So this became the expression for repeating enjoyable things again and again.

Everything is going fine: **SLOW 'N A BEESON TREE Or SLOW LOPE'N A BEESON TREE**

*A **BEESON TREE** was a fine crafted saddle. If you were having a nice day it would be comparable to a nice horse ride in the fresh air.*

Everything or all: **HEELCH**
A large quantity, or the whole amount of something. The expression "The whole cheese" helps you understand the forming of the word.

Exclamation: **EE TAH**
An expression of friendship. Sound similar to the YEEHAW!

Exhausted: **TELLICK**
I don't know the origin of this word but when I'm tired you can "tell I'm licked!"

Eye or Eyeball: **EEBLE**
*"It's hard to be with someone that you don't see **EEBLE** to **EEBLE** with."*

Failure
to meet responsibility: **CHIPPIN**
*Apparently if you don't chip out, to pay bills or other responsibilities, you are a **CHIPPIN**.*

Fall as in failure: **ROOT**

Fancy dressed: **NETTIED**

Fancy/Frilly: **NETTY**
*There was a local woman named Netty. Netty loved lace, the more lace the better. So if you were all **GUSSIED** up in fancy lace or frills you were **NETTY** or **NETTIED**. Example: She was **GUSSIED** in **BAL LOKIN' NETTIES**.*

Fart: **AFE**
Intestinal gas release or to cut the cheese.

Fart: **SLIDER**
*Silent but deadly. That's the worst one!
Use the words in a sentence: He let go of a **SLIDER** that caused my **EEBLES** to **RUDY NEBS**.*

Fawn: **WEE BOSHE**
A little deer.

Fence: **REELF or RELF**
This would be a rail fence.

Fib: **WES**
*Use it in a sentence: George Washington said, "I cannot tell a **WES**." He might have gotten away with it if he'd used Boontling.*

Fiddle or Violin: GOURD

Fiddle player: GOURDER

Fifty Cents or Four Bits: FORBES

Fight,
Getting into a fight: COCK A FISTER ON
*To get into a fight. Also a **LIP-SPLITTIN'**.*
***Sentence:** I wouldn't want to **COCK A FISTER** with Mike Tyson. He might **GORM** my ear.*

Fighters (professional): STIFF HATS
You could tell who these fighters were, they wore derbies.

Fights/Starts them: PICKEM-UP

Fire: A JEFFER or HUGER JEFFER
This would be a nice roaring fire. A local Boonter, Jeff Vestal owned the Missouri House and he was noted for keeping a huge fire in his fire place at all times.

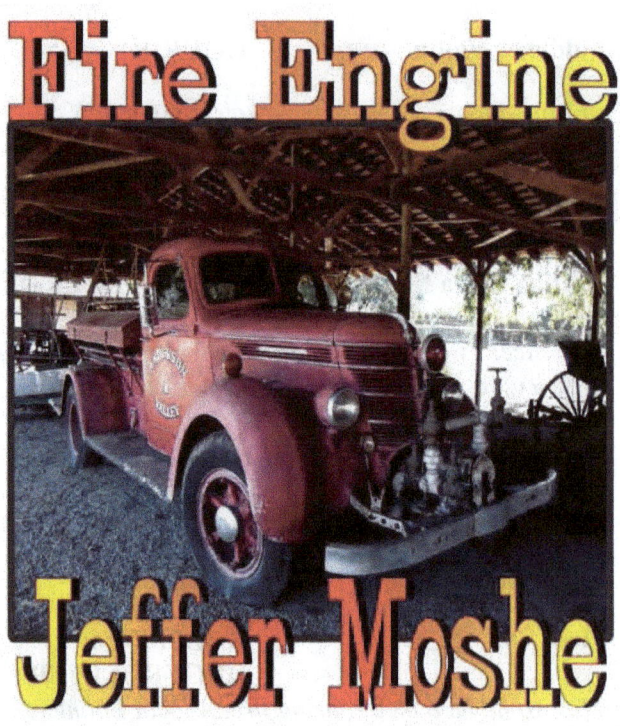

Anderson Valley Fire Engine now on display at the Anderson Valley Historical Museum.

Fish (any kind):   **SEERTLE or SERTLE or SIRTLE**

*Wes 'Deekin' Smoot gave me this definition. When spawning the salmon develop a sore tail or back and after spawning it gets even larger and more swollen. Consequently the "SORE TAIL." The merging of the words has become the word **SEERTLE**.*

Fist: **DUKES**

*This is a common expression since the 1880s. Therefore the expression, "Put up your **DUKES**!"*

Fist-fight: **FISTER or SPILLDUKES**

Flour: **DUMPLIN' DUST**

Focus: **MONTY IN**

*Focus on anything by degrees or to zero in on. There is a really cute picture at the Boonville museum of a pitcher. He is focused on striking the player out. Underneath the picture are the words **MONTY IN**. That is just what he is doing.*

Fog or foggy: **MILKY**

*"The **MILKY** settles in on the **DREARIES** like a blanket."*

Food: **GORMS**
*Now that's **GORMS** for thought!*

Fourth of July: **FOURTH OF JEEL**

Fowl of any kind: **DOM**

Feud: **HANES-CRISPIN**
This was named after two fellows that fought to the death over a gate. Yup, their names were Hanes and Crispin. (pick your battles gentlemen!)

Funeral: **CROAKIN'S**
*I **PIKED** to a Haines and Crispin **CROAKINS** where they buried them in the **BOONT DUSTY**.*

Futile: **KICK ROCKS**
*Similar to a can kicker. It's when you feel something is pointless. The original story goes: Rene McGimsey was married to Marshall McGimsey and he would go to town and get drunk and she would get so mad that she would go around the house kicking everything. And that is where the expression **Can-Kicky** came from originally. As told to me by Bobbie "Wee Bo" Hiatt.*

Gawk, Stare: **TURKEY NECK**
That is when a person is straining their neck around to try and see what's going on.

German: **STRAIGHT NECK**

Girlfriend: **APPLE-HEAD**
*This could be a girl, or a girl friend. There is rumor that it could be for and early Boonter's girl friend that had a small head (but she must have been a delicious **APPLEHEAD** to him!)*

Girl, a young: **APPOLED**
A young girl.

Girl: **KNUCKLEHEAD**
Now this was if the girl was not interesting or pretty. However it's sometimes used as being playful.

Girl (upper-class): **MINK**
This well dressed girl could afford a mink.

Gloves: **HARDIES**
There was quite a lot of handling of tan-oak bark in the Boontling times. The gloves were leather and would get hard and stiff after working with the bark.

Go to Hell: **TOOWEL**

Goat (male): **BILG**
Say the words billy goat really fast and smush it as you do. You'll see this is a shortening of these words.

Good: **BAHL /BALL**
Wes 'Deekin' Smoot told me this story. The word means of excellent quality. There was a brand of shoes called the Ball-Band shoe, with the red ball on the box and I believe the shoes used to have a red ball on the bottom also. If you had a pair of those, you had the finest shoe you could buy. The word has morphed a bit in to this sound of BAHL.

Good quality: **BAHLER**
Anyone or anything of unquestioned excellent quality.

Good Time: **BAL TIDRIC**
This is where a bunch of folks get together and have a great time.

Gossip: **LEW'S 'N LARMERS**
This was the beginning of a poem that became symbolic to gossip.

Grapes: **BOOMTOOKS**

Grapevines: **FRATTEY SHAMS**

Grave or Cemetery: **DUSTIES**
*If someone says you look like you're about to **PIKE** to the **DUSTIES**, you'd better make an appointment with a **SHOVELTOOTH**!*

Gravy: **SOP**
*Would you like some more **BOOS** with that **SOP**?*

Grizzly Bear: **GRIZZLEEBER**

Grapevines Frattey Shams

Haircut: HAIRK or HEDGE
This means to cut a persons hair.

Hairpin Curve: DEVIL'S ELBOW

Handcuffs: BRANDING IRONS
Hard of hearing: TEEBOWED

Hat or Cap: KAYDEE

Hay making time: MOWKEEF
*"You'd better **MOWKEEF** while ol **SOL** is a shinning."*

Hell: OLD DUSTIES
With all these different means attached to the word dusty, I'd better keep my house clean!

Hendy Woods: **BARNEY FLATS**
These woods were first claimed by a man named Joshua Hendy in the late 1800s. He vowed that no one would take and ax and cut them down. In 1958 the State of California purchased them. They are now a protected National Forest, Hendy Woods State Park.

High Country: **BUZZARD**
This boontling word is for folks that lived in the high country or the hills.

Highway 128:   **MACDONALD TO THE SEA**

High School: **THE HEESE**
 Or Elementary School: **WEE HEESE**

Hoard or a Hoarder: **CHIPMUNK**

Homesite or Home: **NOOK** or **ANTHILL**

" *NOOK DULCEY NOOK.*" *Or you could say,*
" *That's a mighty* **BAHL ANTHILL.**"

Horn: **TOOTER**
*Not to be confused with a person that drinks liquor from a **HORN** and goes on a toot!*

Horse: **FUZZ TAIL or SIKE or SIKES**
The word derives from a horse named CYCLONE. Cyclone was reported to be the fastest horse in the valley.

Horse
or traveling by horse: **KILOPPETY**
The word was created by the sound the horse trotting down the road.

Hotel: **HEWTLE, HYOOTLE**

House or Home: **REGION**

Housekeeper: **CASSIE**
This would be a word for a bad housekeeper.

Hug or to hug or smooch: **BARNEY**
This guy Barney appears to get around! This expression was developed about a man named Barney who like to address the women as 'darlin' and often kissed them when saying hello or good-bye.

Huge or Big: **HUGER**

Hungry: **SCOTTIED**
*" I'm so **SCOTTIED** I could **GORM** a **FUZZ TAIL**."*

Hotel Hewtle Hyootle

The Boonville Hotel 2007

Ignorant / naïve: CHUCKLEHEAD

Illegitimate child: BULRUSHER
Someone whose lineage is not immediately known. The word is related to the finding of Moses in the bulrushes.

Inappropriate: EE-FLAT

Indian: BEEKINJ or BEEKINGE
Mingling of the words 'buck injun.'

Infant: SUCK

In love with or Infatuated with: STOOK ON
Just imaging Lionel Richie singing, "Stook on you."

Impotent (male): DREEF

Irritable/nervous: **COLLAR-JUMPY**
The expression, 'getting hot under the collar' comes to mind. This is also a reference to a jumpy horse that reacts negatively to a collar.

Italian: **ITA or ITE**
*A shorting of the Italian name accomplishes this Boont word. Almost every nationality has a Boont name, I'm told. This is the name for an Italian. They lived in a region called **ITALAND** and raised grapes and produced wine and vinegar.*

Jew (male):   **BOARK**

Jingles: **JINGLES or JINKS**
This word would be used for rhymes and song parodies. Do you think the song Jingle Bells was written by a Boontlinger?

Kerosene lantern: **GLIMMER or GLOW WORM**

*Lanterns were often called a **FLOYD HUTSELL**. Now Floyd was a character in the early Boonville that always had a kerosene lantern with him. He was concerned about being caught without light. While there is no recorded history in Boonville of the sun suddenly setting, I do think it's a nice thought to know that there was always light somewhere in Boonville, no matter how dark the night.*

Kill, to: **STRING**

Killed: **STRUNG**
*"The **KAI STRUNG** a **CROPPY**."*

Lamb

Croppy

OR

(the Mexican influence)

Ladies man: **SILENT SEEKER**
*This is a man that goes after the ladies in the strong silent way. You gotta watch out for those quiet ones, **DAMES!***

Lamb: **CROPPY BREGGO** (Mexican influence)
*Did you know that Mary had a **WEE CROPPY** and that its **CROPPY HEDGIN'S** was like **PLENTY WHITE?***

Language: **LING, LINGO, JARGON**

Lantern: **FLOYD HUTSELL**

*Lanterns were often called **FLOYD HUTSELL**. Now Floyd was a character in the early Boonville that always had a Kerosene lantern with him. He was concerned about being caught without light. While there is no recorded history in Boonville of the sun having a tendency to suddenly set, I do think it's a nice thought to know that there was always light somewhere in Boonville no matter how dark the night.*

Lard: **BORP FAT**

Large: **HUGER (hyoojer)**
Anything that is large.

Large Family: **BURT STORK**
Following true to form. When something funny, unusual or happened often the Boonters could come up with a name for it. With having such a large family, his name Burt had become equated with the stork that brought babies.

Large man: **BEEKIN**
This is a Boontling remolding of the words 'big one' after a very large local man.

Laugh at: **HOOT ON**

Laugh loud: **HOOT or BOHOYK**

Laugh loudly: **BOHOIK or HOOTER**
*This is named for a man called **BOHOIK** who had an uninhibited laugh and reportedly could be heard from quite a distance.*
 *"The **WEE HAREEM BOHOIKED** to **DEEK** such a*

*sight and the dish **SHIED** with the spoon."*

Lawsuit: **JAY ESSER**
Named after a Boonter that was in a long legal battle. His initials were J.S.

Leave (to), to quit: **BRANCH or SHIED BRANCHIN'**
Branch out, taking another road or to commit adultery.

Lethargic: **SEEPY**
Someone that is under the effects of drink. Also think of the energy **SEEPING** out of them to help to remember the word.

Letters in the mail: **ALE**

Lie (a whopper): **BOWGLEY**
Use this one for a serious prevarication.

Light Blue Eyes: **GANDER EYES**
This Boontling word meant to have blue eyes like a goose.

Lighthouse on the coast: **BRINEY GLIMMER**
*"Nothing is more reassuring then a **BRINEY GLIMMER** on a **LOG-LIFTER** night.*

Lighthouse Briney Glimmer

Point Arena, California

Loaf, (to): **BUCKEYE**
To loaf or to seek easy tasks and ways of doing things effortlessly.

Loan: **SMEELCH**
While it sounds similar to smell-cheese, it means a small loan, like small change.

Lonely/Deserted: **DOVY-COOEY**

Look: **DEEK**
*"You **DEEKIN'** at me?" Boontling version of Robert DeNiro in Taxi Driver.*

Loss of temper: **GREENY**

Lunch: **LURK**
*"Let's do **LURK**." Hollywood version of Boontling.*

Lunge: **RAMPS**
Also to charge or take a run at.

Machine: MOSHE
*Any mechanical tool or machine might have the Boont word **MOSHE** attached to it.*

Machine: COMOSHE
For grinding sheep shears.

Making Love: RICKY CHOW
*This is a poetic description that was coined about the sound of the twanging bedsprings when a couple would make love. **"RICKY CHOW…RICKY CHOW!"***

Man or Male visitor: KIMMIE or KIMMEY
Sort of sounds like 'come on.'

Man who is young: YINK

Manure: TAISH

Many or Very Many: PLENTY

Marry or get married: **LOCK or LOCKED**
There was an actual **"LOCKING CAKE."** *The cake ingredients consisted of butter, charl, dumplin' dust, doolsey, baking powder and 6 Easters stiffly dreeked, and a tad of vanilla. Yum!*

Here is a wonderful poem written by Donald "Ite" Pardini and reprinted here with his permission for your enjoyment and Boont enrichment.

"Jonesy's Lockin Match"
By Donald "Ite" Pardini in July of 1976.
It concerns the wedding reception of his son, Tony.

Boont was having a lockin match.
It was a bahl July day.
Ite's tweed was tying the knot
And then would slip away.

After the skipe did his job
And the dames all had their cry,
We all shied the Himan's house
For a real ol' Boonter high.

We gathered at the applish nook,
The horns were waiting there.
There was gorms enough for Monk
And music filled the air.

Merle was strumin' oh so hard
And the bootjack roopies too.
Hobbers filled the floor,
A bahl ol' Boionter crew.

Yes everything was bahl,
As the party went into the night.
Not a dame strung her oman
And none of the tweeds did fight.

Then Merle shut the music down.
We passed the hat for more,
And the tweed that played the bass,
Came down upon the floor.

He'd had too much to horn.
He was stepin' plenty high,
And when he walked across the floor,
There was fister in his eye.

And sure as Boonters horn,
When he finally made the door,
He went to spillin' dudes,
Three or four or more.

Now this was all it took,
For I was there to see
Them start the dam best fister
That there will ever be.

Ite tried his best
To break it up right there,
But Pinkey piled right on
And cut off all his air.

Now Ite's oldest tweed
Seen them stringin' dad.
He came at them like Boggs
And gave them all he had.

Then Pinkey threw a beauty
At Ite and scored a hit.
He knocked his snooze a little loose
And he swallowed just a bit.

Then Mossey made a try
To pull them off of Ite.
She caught one in the mouth,
Trying to stop the fight.

She spat out several teeth,
They fell upon the ground.
Then she began to cry,
"Is Dock Dunkle still around?"

The Doc he came to Mossey's side
And checked her molars there.
He harped "Doc's too high to fix them now,
Go home and get your spare."

The fister was almost over,
When Pope so huge and stout
Harped, "All those who bow for fister
Come and try me out."

Too high to even stand,
He's swingin' left and right,
Hitting mostly air,
Ol' Pope was full of fight.

He finally landed one,
The last that he would throw.
He didn't see the punch
That laid him oh so low.

But Pope wasn't done
And when he came around,
His eldom grabbed him by the ears
And raised him off the ground.

Once again upon his feet,
Ol' Pope was reelin' around
A lookin for the kimmey
Who put him on the ground.

Though his eyes were lookin east,
His feet they took him West.
He backed into the cactus parch
And there he came to rest.

Though he bellowed like a bull
When the cactus pricked his skin,
Pope finally gave it up.
The fight was out of him.

Now that it was over,
We all gathered round,
To talk about the fister
And how we knocked them down.

Cecil laughed and harped,
"I even fistered some,
When Mancher bowed behind the bar
I twisted up his thumb.

We guessed there were but only three,
Who didn't swing a blow.
The skipe who wouldn't fight,
And the two who were old and slow.

Though Boonters always fister,
When they get upon a high,
They'll never forget this tidric
As the years go rolling by.
    By Don "Ite" Pardini

Translation of Boont words in
Jonesy's Lockin Match

Verse 1   Lockin match: A wedding

Ite's tweed: Donald Pardini's son Tony who's nickname is Jonesy.

Verse 2   Skipe: Preacher

Shied the himans house - left the preachers house.

The word himan is pronounced with a long I, like highmon.

Verse 3   Applish nook: Apple show building

Enough for Monk: Monk always tried

To crowd in for his part.

Verse 4   Merle: Dean Titus who heads up a

Good western band in Boont

Bootjack Rupies - Cyouti Cowboys:

The name of Dean's Western band.

Verse 5   Strung her oman: Beat her old man.

Verse 7   Horn: To drink.

Fister in his eye: Looking for a fight.

Verse 8	Spilling dudes: Knocking people down.
Verse 10	Pinkey: Nickname for Wayne Hiatt, a local young man.
Verse 11	Like Boggs: Boggs fought like he was just learning to fly.
Verse 13	Mossey: Donna Pardini, Ite's wife.
Verse 14	Dock Dunkle: The local dentist (also an alcoholic).
Verse 16	Pope: Nickname for Dick Sands. A good friend of Pardini's.
Verse 19	His eldom: Pope's wife
Verse 21	Cactus patch: At that time there was a cactus garden about 12 feet by 25 feet just outside of the building where Pope landed.
Verse 24	Cecil: Ite's sister in law and Manchers wife. Bob Pardini, Ite's brother bowed behind the bar making eyes at another girl.

Meat Stew: **LOBO**

Mess: **DOLLISH**
This is used when things are fouled up or really messy.

Milk or Milk a cow: **CHARL**
*This is a sound word. Early Boonter said this was the sound of milking a cow and the milk hitting the can. Also (Spanish version) **LAYCHEE**.*

Mill   **CAM & TOOLEY**
The local mill was called Cam & Tooley. So that became the name of any mill.
*Example: I **OTTO** at the **CAM & TOOLEY**.*

Missouri House: **MEESE HOUSE**

Formerly known as the Anderson Valley Hotel

Mix-up: **KRAISEY or CHRISEY**

Based on two young girls that thought they saw Christ but it was just an itinerant. Their descendents are still spotting His image in toast, windowpanes and potato chips today. (Just kidding).

Money: **HIGS**
The term was **HOG DOLLAR** which is also a **SILVER DOLLAR.**

Mountains: **DREARIES**
Having spent time in Anderson Valley, I understand this expression. Certain times of the year it takes a while in the morning for the fog to burn off the mountains, so it does look dreary.

Muscular: **BUFF**
*This is a current term today for someone that is very strong built. Built like a **BUFF**alo.*

Mustache: **MOOSTY or MOOSTIE**

Mustache (small):   **PAINT BRUSH**

Native of Albion: **ABALONEYITE**

Navarro Residents: **DEEP ENDERS**
The town is located west of Anderson Valley and bordering the Pacific Coast.

Negro: **BOOKER or BOOKER TEE**
After Booker T. Washington.

Nervous / Irritable: **COLLAR-JUMPY**
Referring to a jumpy horse that reacts rejecting a collar.

Nickel: **BUCKEY**
*This is named after the buffalo on the nickel. What song title is this? Put another **BUCKEY** in, in that **BUCKEY MOSHE**. All I want is loving you and music, music, music.*

Night: **NEILCH**

No good: **NONCH**

No more: **NEEMER**

Ocean or Coastal area: BRINEY

Off-key or off-beat: EE-FLAT
This also means inappropriate. If someone says you are EE-FLAT, you are just off!

Old-Age: CODGYHOOD or CODGY or RIDGY

It means old or decrepit.

Old bachelor: GRIZZ
Especially if he lives in squalor.

Old Cow: EELK

Old-fashioned: CODGY
Someone senile, physically decrepit.

Old Man: EELST

Old Man w/ Grey Beard: GREYB or GRABE

Old Woman or Wife: EELD'M

Out of date: **HANGIN'HIGHER 'N BOLLEY'S FIDDLE**

*Bolley was a local that one day without reason just gave up playing his fiddle. This expression can also mean neglected, retired or out of use. Can you imagine the fashion police changing the expression, "That's so last year," to "That outfit was **HANGIN'HIGHER 'N BOLLEY'S FIDDLE!"** Also see definition for DRUNK.*

Over-emotional or Sentimental: **SOMERSETTING**

*What's the name of this song? Gonna take a **SOMERSETTING PIKE**.*

Pancake: **SADDLE BLANKET**

A local woman made pancakes as big as a saddle blanket.

Party: **TIDRICK / TIDRIK**

This can be a group activity or a gathering. Possibly from smushing the words "tea drink."

Actual Bucky Walter on display at the Anderson Valley Historical Museum.

Pay Telephone: **BUCKEY WALTER or WALTER LEVI**

Walter Levi owned the first phone in the valley. As a result of the combination of his name with the Boont name for a nickel "Bucky" we have Bucky Walter.

Peace officer: **HIGH HEEL**

Also used when cited for a violation of the law, or arrest, or put in jail. The origin of the expression: The constable of that time had one leg shorter than the other so he wore a boot that was high-heeled.

Peach: **FUZZY GANNO or FUZZEEK**

Peanut: **GOOBER**

Peel tan bark: **JAY HAWK**

Peeler, the: **JAY HAWKER**

Penmanship: **HEN EGGS 'N OVALS**

*It can also mean to write or practice your Penmanship. This is a very cute expression for sitting down to write. So here I sit **HEN EGGS 'N OVAL** to write this **BOK**.*

I wonder, if computers had been around in those days, would I be sitting down to a frustrated hen, broken yolk and wrist-breakin' board?

Penny: COPPER

People who live on the coast: CHASER OF ABALONES or FOG-EATER

Philo: POLEEKO

Philo is the next town north of Boonville. The building from the Anyhow, Anytime saloon is there. It is currently Libby's Restaurant.

Philo Residence: POLEEKER

This word came from an election in Philo. This is a funny story that "Deekin'" told to me. The men and women had a tendency to cancel out each other with their votes. The women usually voted one way and the men voted the other, making it equal or a POLL EQUALER.

Photographer: CHARLEY WALKER

You can also use this word for a snapshot. You guessed it. Coined after a well respected photographer named Charley Walker.

Picnic: **DOM-GORMIN' TIDRICK**

*This would appear to be a chicken eating get together. Yumm! I wonder if KFC would have the same amount of calories if it were Kentucky Fried **DOM**?*

Picnic Grounds: **DOM-GORMIN' REGION**

This would be the area where you go to eat your chicken!

Pie: **CHARLIE BROWN**

Named after Charlie Brown, a local that loved pie. He ate the pie before meals even breakfast. A man after my own heart. You should ALWAYS eat dessert first so there is room for it!

Pig: **BORP**

*This can also be any pork product. Here's a cute poem I made up. Take your **HOBS** off!*
The Thribble Wee Borps
*This **WEE BORP** went to the **GORMING REGION**.*
*This **WEE BORP** stayed in the **NOOK**.*
*This wee **BORP GORMED** roast beef.*
*And this **WEE BORP** had **NON**.*
*And this **WEE BORP** cried "wee, wee, wee"*
*all the way to the **NOOK**.*

Piper: **TOOTER**
Wes "Deekin'" shared this poem with us.

> *Cerk, Cerk, the tooter's tweed,*
> *Strung a borp and shied.*
> *They gormed the borp*
> *And dreeked wee cerk*
> *And he piked plenty greeneyed.*

Translation:
> *Tom, Tom, the piper's son,*
> *Stole a pig, and away did run!*
> *The pig was eat,*
> *And Tom was beat,*
> *And Tom went crying*
> *Down the street.*

Place, geographical area: **REGION**

Play ball or Baseball: **PLEEBLE**

Pocketknife: **BARLOW**
From the brand name, Barlow.

Pocketwatch (large):   **IKE**
It can also mean turnip but it keeps better time.

Poor: **DEHIGGED**
*Got **HIGS**? You're doing ok! No **HIGS**? Not so good!*

Port wine: **SEEP**

Potato: **BOO**
*Sentence: **The DEHIGGED KIMMIE GORMED BOOS 'N WEEL BOMTOOKS.** Translation: The poor man ate potatoes and wild grapes.*

Potato (sweet): **DOOLSEY BOO**
*"Can I have some **BOO** chips?"*

Preacher: **SKYPE or SKIPE**
It comes from the expression "Sky Preacher."

Pregnancy: **BUCK PASTURE**
This is the advanced stages of pregnancy.

Pregnant: **HEISTED**
*The version from the Pomo Indian's **KAISHBOOK**.*

Professor or Scholar: **GREY-MATTER KIMMIE**

Push or Crowd in: **AB**

Quail: ROOKYTO
This is one of those sound like words. This word was coined for the sound the quail makes.

Quarter, Twenty-five cents: TOOBS

Quit or leave: SHY

Rabbit: BELJEEMER or BELJEEK
BELL-JEEK or BEEL-JEEK

*"Here comes Peter **BELJEEMER, PIKIN'** down the **BELJEEMER** trail!"*

Raccoon: **BOOKER CAT aka slang coon or RACK**
Also for someone with a bad cough.

Rail fence: **RELF or REELF**

Rain or drizzle: **PEERL**

Rainstorm: **LOG-LIFTER**
This would be a heavy one.

Ran off or left: **SHIED**

Rattlesnake: **BLUE TAIL**

Reading glasses: **CHEATERS**
*Nothing better then looking at the **TRUTH** through rose colored **CHEATERS**.*

Rebel Yell or Exclamation: **EE TAH**
Also a sign of friendship.

Red Hair: **BAN**
*This word was originated because of a young man and his father that both had flaming red hair. Their hair was so red that it looked like a red bandana. Ergo: **BAN***

Relatives: **REALS**
Keep it real!

Repeating yourself: **BEE JAY**
Named after a local man who would repeat 'under his breath' what he'd just said verbally...what he just said verbally, oops, it must come with age.

Reprimand / Scolding: **EAR- SETTIN' or ROUTIN' or SET 'N EAR**

Restaurant: **GORM SALE or GORM REGION**

Ride (fast and furious):   **JOE RIDE**
This is very close to the current day expression JOY RIDE.

Rodeo: **BLUEBIRDIN'**
See BUCK

Saddle, a roping: **VISALIA**

Saddle, riding: **BEESON TREE**
Henry Beeson made saddles for Anderson Valley. He had a special design for the wooden base frame, called a tree, over which the leather in saddles was placed. The men that used this saddle would be called a Beeson-tree man. There is a Beeson saddle tree on display at the Boonville Museum.

Saloon: **SALE**
The Anytime later the Anyhow was called the Anytime or Anyhow Sale.

San Francisco: **FRISK**

Sawmill: **AIRTIGHT**
*It means 'no problem.' I wonder if the expression, "He had an **AIRTIGHT** alibi," came from this Boont word?*

School: **WEEHESE**
School for children.

School teacher:	**HEESE TEACH** or **SCHOOLCH** or **SKOOLCH**
Scolding/reprimand:	**EAR-SETTIN'**
Sea lion:	**BRINEY TOMKER**
Sentimental or over emotional:	**SOMERSETTING**

See over emotional.

Con Creek School
Today it is the
Anderson Valley Historical Society Museum.

Sheep:
or BREGGO

CROPPIE OR CROPPY

(Mexican influence)

Sheep (male): **RAMISH**

Sheep Dog: CROPPIE OR CROPPY FETCHER

Sheepshearing session: **CROPPIE OR CROPPY HEDGIN' or SHARSHIN' MATCHES**

Shoe (work shoe): **CLODDY or CLOUDY or plural CLOUDIES**

Shoe (normal) or Dance: **HOB**
*Take your **CLOUDIES** or **HOBS** and go to **HOPLAND**. Show the people at the **TIDRIK** what a **BAHL HOBBER** you are! Don't let the English know or they'll start a show called, "So you **GREYMATTER** you can **HOB**!"*

Shoe (child): **TRILBY**

Shoe Store: **CLOUDY SALE**

Shoot a gun: **BARL**
*Also occurs as the word **KEEBARL** which is the sound it makes when firing a rifle. Or it could come from the word barrel. Whatever the spin-off, it means in 'Boont' to shoot a gun.*

Shout: SPRINGKNEE

Show or Big Show/Entertainment: BEEMSH or BEEMISH

Sick: TONGUE-CUPPY or FLATTENED
It also means bedfast or nauseated.

Silver Dollar: HIG

Simple or inconsequential: TIDREY

Singer, good: WARBLY
*Celine Dion is a **BAHL WARBLY**.*

Skunk: BOARSK

Sleep: SLUG
I sincerely hope this was not how they GOT to sleep!

Slice: MISSIT
To get a slice of something that is so small that if it was smaller you would have missed it.

Slice of anything small: SLIB

Small: SMEEL or WEE

Smooch or hug or to hug: **BARNEY**
It's Barney again. This expression developed about a man named Barney. He loved to greet the women as 'darlin' and often kissed them hello and good bye. Whata guy!

Snow: **PLENTY WHITE**
*Snow storms were called **"PLENTY WHITE TIME."** If the sheep were killed or died they were called **WHITE SPOTS**.*

Sober: **ITCH NEEM'R**
This person no longer has the desire to drink liquor.

Socks (very dirty):   **PICKEM-UP-BILLIES**
*"Take your **PICKEM-UP-BILLLIES** and put them in the laundry!"*

Son: **TWEED**

Spoken: **HARPED**

Spring Season: **BOSHE-BIRD TIME**
Season for birds and deer in large numbers.

Squirrel: SQUEEKYTEEK
Another sound word for squirrels. The early Boonters coined this as the way the squirrel sounded.

Squirrel (Grey): GREYSK

Strawberries: STRAWBS

Stare or to gawk: TURKEY NECK
Cranking your neck around to see what's going on.

Stingy or Miserly: PINCHY

Store up / Collect: CHIPMUNK

Storm (a big one): ROGER or ROAJER

Storm (fairly heavy): TRASHMOVER
*"At first it just **PEERLED** and then it turned into a **TRASHMOVER**!"*

Storyteller: BEARMAN
*The story goes that Allen Cooper a local innkeeper and bear hunter loved to tell tall tales. So if you were a storyteller you'd be tagged a **BEARMAN**.*

Strawberries or Brown beans: **STRAWBS or STREEBS or STRIBS**

*Ok now… first they mix up the **BEARTRACKS** and now they want me to put whipped cream on my beans? That's where I draw the line.*

Strike out: **BIG END**

Stumble: **SHAG or SHAGGISH**

This can also be used to say someone moves awkwardly, clumsy, or is poorly coordinated.

Sulk: **SULL**

Also to make someone angry.

Sun: **OLD SOL**

This is from the Spanish influence.

Sweet: **DOOLSEY or DULCEY**

This can also be used to say sugar or candy.

Sweet Potato: **DOOLSEY BOO DULCEY BOO**

Sworn of liquor: **NONCH NEEMER**

Syrup: **BILL NUNN**

*A local named Bill Nunn loved his syrup. He put it on everything. Move over Mrs. Butterworth hand me some of that **BILL NUNN**.*

Talk: **BULLSH**

This is worthless talk. Reshaping of two words Bull and sh--.

Talk: **HARP**

Talk, chatter: **YATTIN'**

Talk continually: **YABBELOW**

Talk Politics, politicking: **WHITTLIN'**

Talker: **HARPER**

Talkfest: **HARPIN' TIDRICK or SHATTAQUAW**

Tall-tale: **JONNEM or JOHNEM or WHEELERS**

Boonter John M. was a storyteller who liked to s-t-r-e-t-c-h the truth.

Tantrum or Fit: **GREENEY**

Tattletale   **JENNY**

A local school girl named JENNY was a notorious gossip. This is the acclaim given to her.

Teen or Child: **TWEED**

Telephone: **TELEEF'N or TELEFE**

It can also be used to say, call on the phone.

Think, The brain: **GREYMATTER**

Three or Triple: **THRIBBLE**

Threefold: **THRIBFUL**

Three times: **THRIBS**

*"I've told you **THRIBS** to go clean your **SLUGGIN' NOOK!**"*

Throw a rider or unseat: **BLUEBIRD**
See buck. To be 'bluebirded' was to be thrown from a bucking horse. A fallen rider would say, "I got thrown so high a bluebird coulda built a nest on my butt."

Time: **TEEM**

Tired (extremely):   **OSE-DRAGGY**

Tobacco: **TOBE**
*A **TOBE HORNER** is someone who chews but never seems to spit.*

Today: **TEEDEE**

To Hell: **TEE'L**

Toilet or Restroom: **DONICKER or DONAGHER**
Derived from the underworld of the carnival and circus world.

Toilet Paper: **OSE WIPIN'S**

Tom: **SERK**

Tow-truck, local: **BOONT REGION DE-ARKIN' MOSHE**

Tow-truck: **DE-ARKIN' MOSHE**

Train: **IRON MOSHE**
Also used to say locomotive.

Train: **KILOCKETY**
This word was derived by the sound that the train makes.

Transportation: **DEMOSHED**
*If you are **DEMOSHED**, you don't have any transportation.*

Travel: **TREEK or PIKE**
Also used for the word walk.

Trick: **SHARK**
*You can use this one on Halloween, **"SHARK or DOOSEY!"***

Tricking or Fooling: **SHARKING**
*The Boontlingers loved nothing more than to **SHARK** people that came into town. Sometimes they would just get together and have a **SHARKIN' MATCH!** Good times!*

Turbulence, Upset: **SOMERSET aka SOMERSAULT**

See over emotional.

Turnip: **IKE**
It can also mean pocketwatch (large). So if you'd asked for turnips for dinner and they are ticking...

Twenty-two caliber bullet: **SPAT**
Derived from the sound it makes when you shoot the bullet from the gun.

Twenty-five cents/quarter: **TOOBS**

Two of anything: **DUBS**
One single meaning for the word double.

Ukiah: **UKE**

Underground: **BELEEGR'N**
Reworking of the words, 'below ground'. Often used in hunting and pointing out directions. To say the animal has gone underground. Explained to me by "Ite" Pardini.

Understand, Comprehend: **UNDERST**

Upset, turbulence: **SOMERSET aka SOMERSAULT**

Urinate: **KERK or TEEBOUGH**

V

Vest: **LASSIN' JACKET**

Violin or fiddle: **GOURD**

Vote or mark a ballot: **EX**

Walk or to travel: PIKE

Warning: LEEK BEE'N
Simply said, "Look behind," to which someone says, "Huh?"

Water: RUDY NEBS
In the early 1900s, Rudy Nebs a famous cartoonist, came to the Boonville. When he tasted the water from well at the then Andersen Inn he was impressed by its taste. He offered the hotel a ton of money for the well. They refused. He admired the spirit of the people for that so he gave the water his name. Sadly, the well at the Missouri house is no longer in use.

Watermelon: SIFTER
If it didn't have the seeds it would sort of look like one.

Wealthy or having money: **HIGGY or HIGHPOCKETY or HIGH POCKETS**

*The richest man in the region was also the tallest. It's simple math, him being the tallest that made his pockets taller than anyone else. Ergo: **HIGHPOCKETY***

Wedding: **LOCKIN' or LOCKING**

Wedding or Engagement: **LOCKIN' MATCH**

Well dressed: **GUSSIED**
*The bride was **GUSSIED** in **BAL LOKIN' NETTIES.***

Whipping or Beating: **DREEKIN'**

Whiskey: **BLUE GRASS of SKEE**

Whiskey Drinker: **SKEE HORNER**

Whole Cheese, the: **HEELCH**
*I can see it now, **CHARLIE WALKERS** everywhere will all be saying, "Okay now, smile and say **HEELCH**!"*

Wild:	**WEEL**
Wild cat:	**WILK**
Wine:	**FRATTY or SEEP**
Wine: *Wine drinker.*	**SEEP HORNER**
Wine (red wine):	**ROSY**
Winter:	**TRASH MOVER**
Winter Storm: *This is used for a strong winter storm.*	**LOG LIFTER**
Wild or Crazy:	**CRAYZEEK**
Wild Cat:	**WEELK**
Wild Cat/Bob Cat area:	**WEELK REGION**
Woman: *This is an expression for a woman who is unkempt.*	**STRINGY-HAIR-'N-WRINKLE-SOCKS**

Woman/Wife: **DAME or DAMES**

Here is a fun story told many years ago in Boonville in Boontling about "The Eeld'm and the Borp." For you beginners it is,
   "The Old Woman and the Pig."

An eeld'm, found some forbes and buckeys, and felt highpockety. So she piked to Boont and used her higs for borp.

On her way region, the eeld'm had to pike over a relf. But borp wouldn't pike, and she couldn't jape him to region and she wanted chiggrel.

Soon a hareem piked by, and the eeld'm harped, "Hareem, hareem, chiggrel borp, borp won't jump relf and pike region, and I'll get no chiggrel." But hareem noned.

Eeld'm got cocked and harped to a stick, "Stick, stick, dreek hareem, hareem won't chiggrel borp, borp won't jump relf and pike region, and I'll get no chiggrel." But stick noned.

Soon she met a jeffer. Still in a greeny, she harped,
   "Jeffer, jeffer, ark stick, stick won't dreek hareem, hareem won't chiggrel borp, borp won't jump relf and pike region, and I'll get no chiggrel." But jeffer noned.

To make a long story short, the eeld'm soon met a briny and asked it to quench jeffer. But briny noned.

Then she found a broady and asked it to horn briny. But broady noned!

Then she found a broady kimmey and asked him to kill broady. But broady kimmey noned!

So eeld'm pike to a rope and asked it to hang kimmey, but rope noned!

Then eeld'm found a rat and asked it to chiggrel rope. But rat noned!

She piked on to a pusseek, and pusseek harped, "If you'll pike to yon broady and charl her for me, I'll chiggrel the rat."

So she piked to the broady. But broady harped, "If you'll pike to the haystack and fetch me some chiggrel, I'll charl myself for pusseek.

So eeld'm did what broady asked, and broady chiggreled and pusseek horned. Then pusseek began to kill rat, rat began to chiggrel rope, rope began to hang broady kimmey, broady kimmey began to kill broady, broady began to horn briny, briny began to quench jeffer, jeffer began to ark stick, stick began to dreek hareem, hareem began to chiggrel borp, borp began to jump relf and pike region, and eeld'm got her chiggrel!

Author unknown

Okay, you've almost graduated "Boontling School" you should be getting close to understanding all the stories and poems!

Wool: **CROPPY HEDGIN'S**
This is a sheepshearing session.

Work hard: **OT or OTTO**
The term was started because there were so many immigrant workers named OTTO that the name became just the same as the word work.

Worker: **CHUCK ROBINSON**
Named for a local that was always late and behind.

Working: **OT'N or OTTOING**

Worrisome or doubtful: **SKIDDLEY**
*"April 15th is always a **SKIDDLEY TEEM**."*

Wreck: **ARKIN' TIDRICK**
This is any sort of a wreck or destructive project or auto or collision.

Wreck, damage or destroy: **ARK**

Write, to: **HEN EGGS 'N OVALS**

Practice my penmanship or writing.

Written: **HEN EGGED 'N OVALED**

Yes: **YIBE**

May I see a show of hands or a resounding **YIBE!?**

Yorkville Residents: **HIGH ROLLERS**

This is smallest town in the Anderson Valley region, Located 10 miles east of Boonville. In the early days The young men of Yorkville would come to the dances in Boonville.

However, the road was long and dirty so they didn't want their pants to get dirty so they would roll up their pants and put overalls over them and go to the dance. In their excitement to get into the dance with the **DAMES** *they would forget to roll their pant legs down. So everyone knew they were the* **HIGH ROLLERS** *from Yorkville.*

Time to test your GREYMATTER!
As you can see in most cases the Boontling word is sprinkled throughout the sentence.

1. MOSHE STRUNG the KIMMIE.
2. WHITTLE a SLIB by the JEFFER.
3. Got enough ZEESE for a GORMIN' TIDRIC.
4. You from BELK?
5. I SHIED the HOB.
6. I'm too CODGY.
7. There was a huge FISTER.
8. He PIKED to the DUSTIES.
9. It was a NONCH BLOOD'N HAIR.
10. Thou shalt not commit BRANCHIN'.
11. We saw an 'ol BEARK stalking a CROPPY."
12. PIKIN' to the TURKEY SHACK.
13. I GORMED the whole bag of BOO chips.
14. That bridge looks too RIDGY to cross.
15. If I don't SHY to the SLUGGIN' REGION soon, I may as well set me a JEFFER and GORM BOWRP and EASTERS."
16. Billy was put in the corner for NONCH HARPIN'.
17. He was DREEKED nearly to death.
18. GORMING a BAHL FLORIE.
19. That SEERTLE was SOCKER!

20. I went to Vegas HIGHPOCKETY but came back DEHIGGED.
21. I'm NICKELONKED.
22. The eternal question is, which came first, the DOMINECKER or the EASTER?
23. KEEMWUN KEEMLE!
24. When I first heard Boont harped I was so JIMHEADY.
25. CHIGGRUL NOOK IS STRUNG.
26. It gets mighty DOVY-COOEY in the COW SKULLY REGION.
27. If you HORN don't JAPE.
28. Put an EASTER under your foot and JAPE safely.
29. I'm a very BAHL JAPER.
30. I can't believe I GORMED the HEELCH!
31. It's hard to be with someone that you don't see EEBLE to EEBLE with.
32. Would you like some more BOOS with that SOP?
33. NOOK DULCEY NOOK.
34. That's a mighty BAHL ANTHILL.
35. I'm so SCOTTIED I could GORM a FUZZ TAIL.
36. The WEE HAREEM BOHOIKED to DEEK such a sight and the dish SHIED with the spoon.

37. Nothing is more reassuring then a BRINEY GLIMMER on a LOG-LIFTER night.
38. You DEEKIN' at me?
39. The DEHIGGED KIMMIE GORMED BOOS 'N WEEL BOMTOOKS.
40. Can I have some BOO CHIPS?
41. Take your PICKEM-UP-BILLLIES and put them in the laundry!
42. At first it just PEERLED and then it turned into a TRASHMOVER!"
43. I've told you THRIBS to go clean your SLUGGIN' NOOK!
44. SHARK or DOOSEY!
45. The bride was GUSSIED in BAL LOKIN' NETTIES.

ANSWERS

1. The guys' car broke down.
2. Sit by the fire and talk some politics.
3. There is enough coffee for an eating get together.
4. You from Bell Valley?
5. I left the dance.
6. I'm too old.
7. There was a big fight.
8. He died.
9. It was a really bad accident.
10. Thou shalt not commit adultery.
11. We saw a bearcat stalking a sheep.
12. Going to get some alcohol.
13. I ate the whole bag of potato chips.
14. That bridge looks too old to cross.
15. If I don't go to sleep pretty soon I might as well light a fire and cook some bacon and eggs.
16. Billy was put in the corner for using bad language.
17. He was beat nearly to death.
18. Eating a very good biscuit.
19. That fish was a big one!
20. I went to Vegas rich but came back poor.
21. Out of nickels to play with.

22. The eternal question is, which came first, the chicken or the egg?
23. Come one, come all!
24. When I first heard Boontling spoken I was so confused.
25. The cupboard is bare.
26. It gets mighty lonely in the desolate area.
27. If you drink don't drive.
28. Put and egg under your foot and drive safely.
29. I'm a very good driver.
30. I can't believe I ate the whole thing!
31. It's hard to be with someone that you don't see eyeball to eyeball with.
32. Would you like some more potatoes with that gravy?
33. Home Sweet Home.
34. That's a mighty nice home.
35. I'm so hungry I could eat a horse.
36. The little dog laughed to see such a sight and the dish ran away with the spoon.
37. Nothing is more reassuring then a lighthouse on a stormy night.
38. You lookin' at me?
39. The poor man ate potatoes and wild grapes.
40. Can I have some potato chips?
41. Take your dirty sox and put them in the laundry!

42. At first it just sprinkled and then it turned in to a storm!
43. I've told you three times to go clean your bedroom.
44. Trick or treat!
45. The bride was dressed up in her wedding clothes.

Judy Belshe-Toernblom © 2007
2nd Edition
revised: Wednesday, April 25, 2010

Come one, come all to Boonville!

Keemwun, keemle to Boont!

To order books for your group or party:
(562) 430-2299
or email
JudyBelshe@aol.com

www.ingramcontent.com/pod-product-compliance
Lightning Source LLC
Chambersburg PA
CBHW071133090426
42736CB00012B/2112